Brilliant
BIRTHDAY CAKES

JOANNA FARROW

Making novelty cakes for children is great fun. Youngsters are less critical than adults and are easily impressed by bold colours and simple designs that resemble animals, prehistoric monsters or fairy-tale scenes.

In this book you'll find cakes for children of all ages. Some can be assembled in less than an hour, while other, more elaborate, creations are designed for those who have the time, and inclination, to get thoroughly absorbed.

The cakes are all made from Madeira sponge and decorated with simple icings that children love, such as sugarpaste and buttercream. Basic cake-making information is given, together with all the icing recipes and instructions you need for shaping and decorating the cakes. Helpful hints and colourful photographs throughout the book will help you choose the cake you want to make and guide you step-by-step, towards its completion.

Whichever cake you choose, you can be sure it will be greeted with smiles of delight!

CONTENTS

BASIC CAKE MAKING

MADEIRA CAKE

For ingredients, tin sizes, baking times and flavourings, see the chart. Although this is not the traditional method for making a Madeira cake, it is very quick and easy. If you don't have an electric whisk or mixer, cream the butter or margarine and sugar together first, then gradually beat in the eggs and finally fold in the sifted flour and any flavouring.

1 Preheat the oven to 160°C (325°F/ Gas 3). Grease and line the required tin. Put the softened butter or margarine, sugar, eggs and sifted flour in a large bowl. Add the chosen flavouring, if desired (see chart).

2 Beat with an electric whisk for about 2 minutes or until the mixture is pale and fluffy.

3 Turn the mixture into the prepared tin and level the surface. Bake in the oven for the time stated in the chart or until the cake is firm to the touch and a skewer inserted in the centre comes out clean. Leave to cool slightly in the tin, then turn out on to a wire rack and leave to cool completely. Wrap the cake tightly in foil until ready to decorate.

MADEIRA CAKE QUANTITIES CHART

Round tin	15cm (6 inch)	18cm (7 inch)	20cm (8 inch)	23cm (9 inch)	25cm (10 inch)
Square tin	13cm (5 inch)	15cm (6 inch)	18cm (7 inch)	20cm (8 inch)	23cm (9 inch)
Butter or margarine, softened	125g (4oz)	185g (6oz)	315g (10oz)	440g (14oz)	500g (1lb)
Caster sugar	125g (4oz/½ cup)	185g (6oz/¾ cup)	315g (10oz/1¼ cups)	440g (14oz/1¾ cups)	500g (1lb/2 cups)
Eggs	2	3	5	7	8
Self-raising flour	185g (6oz/1½ cups)	250g (8oz/2 cups)	375g (12oz/3 cups)	500g (1lb/4 cups)	625g (1¼lb/5 cups)

FLAVOURINGS

Ground mixed spice	1 tsp	1 tsp	1½ tsp	2 tsp	3 tsp
Citrus (grated rind of lemon, orange or lime)	1	2	3	4	5
Chopped mixed nuts	30g (1oz/¼ cup)	60g (2oz/½ cup)	90g (3oz/¾ cup)	125g (4oz/1 cup)	155g (5oz/1¼ cups)
Baking time	1–1¼ hours	1¼–1½ hours	1½–1¾ hours	1¾–2 hours	2 hours

TO LINE A CAKE TIN
Place the tin on a piece of greaseproof or non-stick paper and draw around it, then cut out the shape just inside the drawn line. Cut a strip of paper that is as long as the circumference of the tin and 2.5cm (1 inch) deeper. Make a 2.5cm (1 inch) fold along one long edge of the strip and snip the folded portion from the edge to the fold at 2.5cm (1 inch) intervals. Position the strip around the inside of the greased tin with the snipped edge flat on the base. Place the cut-out piece of paper in the base, then grease the paper.

Fit the paper inside the tin, making sure the snipped area lies flat on the base.

COOK'S HINTS
If possible, always make cakes the day before decorating them as they cut better. This is particularly important when shaping novelty cakes. Well wrapped in foil, a Madeira will keep for up to a week. Freeze if keeping for longer.

COOK'S HINT
Cakes can be made in hexagonal tins using the same quantities of ingredients and cooking times as those given for round tins of the same size.

BASIC ICING RECIPES

SUGARPASTE

You can use either bought or home-made sugarpaste for the cakes in this book. Bought sugarpaste, sold 'ready-to-roll', has a similar taste and texture to the homemade version but might work out slightly more expensive if used in large quantities. The following recipe makes sufficient sugarpaste to cover a 15–18cm (6–7 inch) cake.

Makes 500g (1lb)
1 egg white
6 tsp liquid glucose
500g (1lb/3 cups) icing sugar
icing sugar for dusting

Put the egg white and liquid glucose in a bowl. Gradually beat in the icing sugar until the mixture becomes too stiff to stir. Turn it out on to a surface sprinkled with icing sugar and knead in the remaining icing sugar until the mixture forms a smooth, stiff paste. Use immediately, or wrap tightly in plastic food wrap and store in a cool place for up to 1 week. (If storing for more than a few hours, wrap in a double thickness of plastic wrap, or put wrapped sugarpaste in a sealed polythene bag.)

COOK'S HINTS

If your homemade sugarpaste is sticky when you roll it out, work in more icing sugar and roll again. If it is too dry, knead in a little water.

Some varieties of bought sugarpaste are very soft and sticky. These, too, benefit from a little extra icing sugar being kneaded in before rolling and shaping.

ROYAL ICING

Used for flat icing and piping, royal icing is mostly required for tradition-ally decorated celebration cakes, but is also used on some novelty cakes. To prevent a crust forming once made, cover the surface of the icing with plastic food wrap, place a damp cloth over the wrap, then cover the bowl with a second piece of plastic wrap. Well sealed, royal icing will store for several days. The following recipe makes sufficient royal icing for most decorative purposes.

Makes 250g (8oz/1 cup)
1 egg white
250g (8oz/1½ cups) icing sugar,
sifted

Lightly whisk the egg white in a bowl, then gradually beat in the icing sugar, beating well after each addition until the icing forms soft peaks.

BUTTERCREAM

Buttercream is used for covering sponge cakes and gâteaux, and is par-ticularly popular for children's novelty cakes. It can be piped or spread, flavoured and coloured, and is very easy to work with. The following recipe makes sufficient buttercream to sandwich and cover the top of a 20cm (8 inch) sponge cake.

Makes 375g (12oz/1½ cups)
125g (4oz) butter or margarine,
softened
250g (8oz/1½ cups) icing sugar
2 tsp boiling water

Put the butter or margarine in a bowl and sift over the icing sugar. Beat together until creamy. Add the water and beat again until soft and pale.

BUTTERCREAM FLAVOURINGS

Citrus Add the finely grated rind of 1 orange, lemon or lime.
Coffee Add 2 tsp coffee essence.
Chocolate Add 30g (1oz) sifted cocoa powder.
Almond Add 1 tsp almond essence.

COOK'S HINT

Buttercream naturally has a dark yellow colour, making it less easy to colour than other icings. If you want a richly coloured buttercream, substitute white vegetable fat for the butter or margarine.

APRICOT GLAZE

This can be made in large quantities and stored in the refrigerator for sev-eral weeks. It is used to brush over a cake before covering with sugarpaste. If a recipe uses more than 3 tbsp apri-cot glaze, don't forget to increase the amount of water required in propor-tion to the jam.

3 tbsp apricot jam
1 tsp water

Put the jam and water in a saucepan and heat gently until the jam has melted. Press through a small sieve using a teaspoon.

SUGARPASTE TECHNIQUES

COLOURING SUGARPASTE

KNEADING IN COLOUR
Place the measured quantity of sugar-paste on a surface dusted with corn-flour and knead lightly until smooth. Using a cocktail stick, dot liquid colouring on to the sugarpaste, then knead in until completely blended.

Always add colours sparingly as some are much stronger than others. For pastel shades, the icing might need only the smallest amount, while several additions of colour might be needed for deeper shades. Once the required colour is achieved, keep the sugarpaste tightly wrapped in a double thickness of plastic food wrap until ready to use.

MARBLING
This is achieved by only partially blending the colouring into the sugar-paste. Dot the icing sparingly with the chosen colour, as above. Roll the icing to a long, thick sausage shape, then fold the ends to the centre and dot with a little more colour. Reroll to a thick sausage and fold the ends in once again. Repeat the rolling and folding, without adding any more colour, until the colour starts to show in thin streaks. Add more colour, and repeat the rolling and folding process, if stronger marbling is required, but take care not to overwork the sugarpaste, resulting in a uniform colour all over.

Once sufficiently marbled, roll out the sugarpaste and use to cover a cake or board, as required.

SECURING DECORATIONS
There are two simple methods of securing decorations on a cake.

SECURING WITH WATER
For decorations that are cut out and secured to the cake while still soft, such as the coloured trucks on the Travelling Trucks cake (see page 14), use a small paintbrush that has been lightly dampened with water. Dampen either the underside of the piece of icing to be secured, or the area of cake to which the decoration is to be attached, whichever is the easier method.

SECURING WITH ICING
Decorations that are left to harden before being applied to a cake, such as flowers and leaves, are best secured with a little icing. If the cake uses royal icing, use small dots of this to secure. Alternatively, mix a little icing sugar with a dash of water to make a firm paste. Dot the underside of the decoration with the icing and secure in position.

Using a cocktail stick prevents you adding too much colour at once.

Rolling and folding, rather than kneading, creates a 'marbled' effect.

> #### COOK'S HINTS
> *When securing decorations with water, do not 'wet' the icing, otherwise the shapes will not adhere. When securing with icing, only the smallest amount is required. Large blobs look unsightly.*

USING TEMPLATES

A few of the cake designs in this book use a template to create a particular sugarpaste shape. To use the template, first trace the outline on to a piece of greaseproof or non-stick paper, then cut it out.

On a surface dusted with cornflour, roll out sugarpaste in the chosen colour. Gently rest the paper template over the icing. Using a sharp knife, cut around the template, then lift it away. Use as required.

Paper templates can be used to cut out any decorative shape you choose.

COVERING A CAKE WITH SUGARPASTE

The amount of sugarpaste required varies from cake to cake. The recipes in this book give the exact quantity required for each cake.

Lightly knead the required amount of sugarpaste to soften it slightly. Dust a work surface with icing sugar and roll out the sugarpaste to a round or square 7.5cm (3 inches) larger than the diameter of the cake. Lift the sugarpaste on the rolling pin and lay it over the top of the cake. Dust the palms of your hands lightly with cornflour and smooth the sugarpaste over the top and down the sides of the cake, easing it gently to fit around the sides. If it forms folds and creases, keep smoothing the paste to eliminate them. Trim off any excess paste around the base of the cake.

COOK'S HINTS

An icing smoother gives a beautiful finish to a cake covered with sugarpaste. Lightly dust the smoother with cornflour, then gently move it over the surface of the sugarpaste, using a circular 'ironing' action, until the icing is smooth and silky.

Lift the rolled-out sugarpaste on the rolling pin and drape it over the cake.

Smooth the sugarpaste with your hands until you have a perfect finish.

TO MAKE A PAPER PIPING BAG

Cut a 25cm (10 inch) square of grease-proof paper, then cut the square in half diagonally to make two triangles. Holding one triangle with its longest side away from you, fold the right-hand point over to meet the bottom point, curling the paper round to make a cone shape.

Fold the left-hand point over the cone and bring all three points together. Fold the points over twice to secure. Cut off 1cm (½ inch) of the tip and fit with a piping tube.

Curl the paper round in a cone, bringing the right-hand point to the bottom point.

When the folding is completed, all three points of the triangle should be together.

NOVELTY CAKE TECHNIQUES

FINISHING JOINS IN SUGARPASTE

With a little practice, joins in sugar-paste can be smoothed out completely. Lightly dampen the edges that are to meet, then overlap them very slightly. Rub the edges together, using your fingertips. If the icing starts to feel sticky, dust your fingertips very lightly with cornflour and continue to rub over the join until it disappears.

> **COOK'S HINT**
>
> *You can only hide a join successfully when the icing is freshly rolled or moulded. Once it begins to harden, it quickly forms a crust which cannot be completely concealed.*

LINING EMPTY FOOD CANS

For tubular-shaped cakes, such as the Dream Castle (see page 19) and the Messy Paints cake (see page 26), empty food cans make perfect baking tins. Remove both ends from the can, then wash and dry thoroughly.

Place the can on a piece of grease-proof or non-stick paper and draw around it. Cut out the paper circle, just inside the drawn line. Cut a strip of paper the circumference of the can and 1cm (½ inch) deeper. Make a 1cm (½ inch) fold along one long edge, then snip the paper along the folded portion, from the edge to the fold, at 1cm (½ inch) intervals.

Brush the inside of the can with melted margarine. Bring the two short ends of the paper strip together and push into the can. Place the can on a greased baking sheet so that the snipped portion of paper rests flats on the sheet. Fit the circle of paper in the base. Brush the paper with more melted margarine.

The can is now ready to be filled with mixture. Level the surface carefully and do not overcook.

'PEAKING' BUTTERCREAM

Buttercream is perfect for creating a quick and easy 'sea' effect. Colour some buttercream blue, then spread it on to the surface using a palette knife. Once thickly covered, rough up the buttercream using the back of a teaspoon. For 'foaming waves', coat the back of a clean teaspoon with plain buttercream, then touch the blue peaks to leave white tips.

Continue rubbing with your fingertips until the join is smoothed over.

Line the sides of the can so the snipped paper protrudes at the bottom end.

Use the back of a teaspoon to pull the icing up into peaks.

ADDING CANDLES

If there's no room on the cake for candles and holders, or you feel they will spoil the look of the cake, they can be used to decorate the cake board instead.

Candle holders can be made out of sugarpaste. Roll small balls in your chosen colour and flatten them slightly. Secure to the board with a dampened paintbrush. Dampen the bases of the candles and press them into the balls of sugarpaste. Alternatively, cut out small flower or star shapes using a cutter, and secure in the same way.

ICING CUT-OUTS

One of the simplest ways to decorate a child's cake is to cover the cake with simple cut-outs made using biscuit, numeral, alphabet or novelty-shape cutters of various sizes.

Thinly roll out some sugarpaste in your chosen colour on a surface dusted with cornflour. Dip the cutters in cornflour to prevent sticking, then cut out shapes. Dampen the underside of each shape and secure to the cake. By using a selection of cutters, or cutting shapes by hand, you can build up complete sugarpaste pictures, such as a clown's face, a simple house, a train, a car, etc.

> ### COOK'S HINT
> *When dampening sugarpaste shapes to secure them, use very little water, otherwise the cut-outs will slide around and the colours may run.*

CUTTING CAKES INTO SHAPES

Many novelty cakes are made using a cake that has been cut to a particular shape. If possible, make the cake a day in advance as it will then be firmer and easier to cut.

Use a sharp, slender knife for cutting, and work with a sawing action. When a perfect vertical cut is needed, make sure the knife is held in an upright position.

Decorative sugarpaste shapes make attractive candle holders.

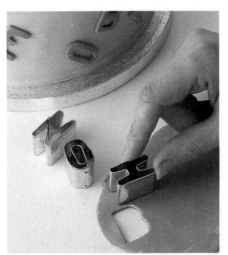

Cut-out shapes of all sorts can be used to make a quick and easy decoration.

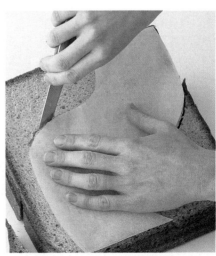

Use a paper template as a guide when cutting cake into shapes.

Jungle Cake

Animals of any description appeal to most children. This simple creation, in buttercream and sugarpaste, is perfect for younger boys and girls.

Serves 16

CAKE
two 15cm (6 inch) round Madeira cakes (see page 2)

FILLING AND DECORATION
1kg (2lb) Sugarpaste (see page 3)
yellow, red, black, brown, pale green and dark green food colourings
cornflour for dusting
500g (1lb/2 cups) chocolate Buttercream (see page 3)

EQUIPMENT
fine paintbrush
cocktail sticks
23cm (9 inch) round silver cake board
palette knife

1 To make the giraffes, colour 60g (2oz) of the sugarpaste yellow. Trace the giraffe template (below) on to greaseproof or non-stick paper and cut it out. Thinly roll out the yellow sugarpaste on a surface dusted with cornflour. Lay the template on the sugarpaste and cut around it. Make another giraffe, then turn the template over and cut out another two facing the other way. (One set acts as a spare.)

2 Using a knife, cut down between the horns to separate them. Roll small balls of yellow sugarpaste and secure to the ends of the horns with a dampened paintbrush. Dampen the ends of wooden cocktail sticks and lay them under the base of each giraffe. Press down lightly to secure. Transfer to a sheet of greaseproof or non-stick paper and leave for at least 24 hours to harden. Wrap the remaining sugarpaste in plastic food wrap.

3 Using a fine paintbrush and slightly diluted colourings, paint red markings and black facial features on the giraffes.

4 Level the surface of one cake by cutting off any peak formed during baking. Place the cake on the board. Spread with a little buttercream, then cover with the second cake. Completely spread the top and sides with the remaining buttercream, smoothing it as flat as possible with the palette knife.

continued on page 10

COOK'S HINTS

Small, round, bought cakes are perfect for this. Stack three together as they tend to be shallower than homemade sponges.

If you only have one green food colouring, make half the treetops, then darken the remaining green sugarpaste by adding extra green and a little black food colouring.

If liked, cut out extra giraffe shapes and press together to make double-sided giraffes with the cocktail sticks in the middle. Paint markings on both sides.

After cutting out the giraffes, use a knife to cut the 'horn' sections into two.

Use a fine paintbrush to paint red markings and black eyes and mouths on the giraffes.

5 Colour 500g (1lb) of the remaining sugarpaste brown. Roll out a little to a long sausage, roughly the depth of the cake. Flatten slightly, then cut slits down one end and open out slightly for branches. Make bark markings with the tip of a knife and secure to the side of the cake. Make more trees in the same way, varying the size of each.

6 Colour 155g (5oz) of the remaining sugarpaste pale green and another 155g (5oz) dark green (see Cook's Hints). Roll out a small ball of one colour to a 12cm (4½ inch) round. Pull up the edges and pinch together. Turn the piece of sugarpaste over and press into position on the top of the cake to resemble a tree.

Make more treetops in the same way. Arrange them on the cake so the colours alternate and overlap slightly.

7 Roll small balls of white icing and position around the cake in pairs to resemble peering eyes.

8 Colour more trimmings grey and shape elephants' trunks. Press into the buttercream and secure to the trees with a dampened paintbrush.

9 Make brightly coloured snakes from the remaining trimmings. Secure to the tree trunks. Make snakes' eyes as above. Paint the centres of the eyes, and snake markings with a fine paintbrush and black food colouring.

Cut long, shallow lines in the 'tree trunks' to represent bark.

Position the green 'treetops' with the edges of the pieces tucked underneath.

Aqua Zoom

Water shoots or flumes are now a highlight of many leisure pools. This cake should appeal to most children, even if they've never had a go on one.

1 Level the surface of the cake by cutting off any peak formed during baking. Using a large, sharp knife, cut the cake in half from one top edge to the opposite lower edge. Turn the upper piece round so that the thin sides are together, creating a slope.

2 Using a knife, cut out an inverted 's' shape from the cake. Reserve one of the large trimmed sections.

3 Use a third of the buttercream, and 4 tbsp of the jam to sandwich the split cakes together. Press the remaining jam through a sieve to remove any pieces, then brush it over both pieces of the cake.

4 Place the large cake towards the back of the cake board. Roll out 1kg (2lb) of the sugarpaste on a surface dusted with cornflour to a 36cm (14 inch) circle. Lay this over the large cake and smooth down the sides, easing it to fit. Trim off excess icing around the base. Use the trimmings and another 375g (12oz) sugarpaste to cover the small piece of cake. Place on the cake board.

5 Using a fine paintbrush and diluted blue food colouring, paint the sides of the cakes with stripes for a tiled effect.

6 Colour another 375g (12oz) sugarpaste blue. Roll a little under the palms of your hands to a long sausage. Secure this down the centre of the large cake, then press all along to a point. Roll out the remaining blue icing and cut out two strips, each 30 × 7.5cm (12 × 3 inches).

Serves 16

CAKE
23cm (9 inch) square Madeira cake (see page 2)

ICING AND DECORATION
500g (1lb/2 cups) Buttercream (see page 3)
7 tbsp strawberry or raspberry jam
2kg (4lb) Sugarpaste (see page 3)
cornflour for dusting
blue, flesh, red, green and yellow food colourings
plastic greenery, e.g. palm trees, foliage, etc.

EQUIPMENT
33cm (13 inch) square silver cake board
palette knife
fine paintbrush
cocktail stick

Use a large, sharp knife to cut the cake into a rough inverted 's' shape.

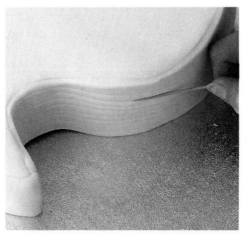

Before painting stripes on the side of the cake, mark guidelines with a cocktail stick.

7 Dampen the flat surface of the cake. Fit one blue strip down one side of the shoot, so that one side rests on the blue ridge in the centre. Curve the other side of the strip up, supporting it, if necessary, with crumpled absorbent kitchen paper. Position the second strip on the other side of the shoot.

8 Set aside 2 tbsp of the remaining buttercream, and colour the rest blue. Spread this over the board with a palette knife, peaking it in some areas. Spread a thin covering of blue buttercream down the shoot. Peak the blue buttercream around and down the shoots with the reserved white buttercream (see page 6).

9 Colour half the remaining sugarpaste with flesh colouring. Roll a little to a thin sausage, about 6cm (2½ inches) long.

Flatten slightly, then make a 2cm (¾ inch) cut from each end towards the centre. Mould the cut sections into outstretched arms and legs.

10 Place the figure halfway down one of the shoots. Add a small head and paint a swimsuit on to the body using a fine paintbrush.

11 Make more figures in the same way. For the boy leaving the shoot, support the back with a cocktail stick, then lean it against the shoot with the feet touching the water. Shape two or three 'head and shoulder' figures in the water. Add hair using coloured sugarpaste.

12 Use the remaining sugarpaste to shape extra decorations, such as a beach ball. Add plastic palm trees, or other foliage, as required.

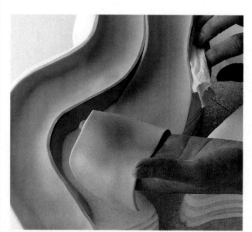

Pieces of kitchen paper can be used to support the sugarpaste while it hardens.

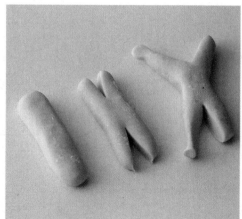

Shape simple sugarpaste figures, then paint on the details when in position.

Travelling Trucks

Simple shapes in bright colours appeal to very young children. This theme would work equally well with cars or trains.

Serves 16

CAKE
20cm (8 inch) round Madeira cake (see page 2)

FILLING AND DECORATION
7 tbsp strawberry or raspberry jam
125g (4oz / ½ cup) Buttercream (see page 3)
1.5kg (3lb) Sugarpaste (see page 3)
cornflour for dusting
green, red, brown, blue, black and yellow food colourings
candles

EQUIPMENT
25cm (10 inch) round silver cake board
fine paintbrush

1 Cut the cake horizontally in half. Place the lower half on the cake board and spread with 4 tbsp of the jam. Spread the jam with the buttercream, then cover with the second layer.

2 Sieve the remaining jam to remove any pieces, then brush over the top and sides of the cake.

3 Roll out 1kg (2lb) of the sugarpaste on a surface dusted with cornflour and use to cover the cake (see page 5).

4 Colour another 125g (4oz) of the sugarpaste green. Reserve a little, then roll out the remainder to a strip that is as long as the circumference of the cake. Cut one edge straight and the other in a wavy line. Dampen the bottom edge of the cake with water, then wrap the strip around the cake and secure.

5 Trace the template (below) on to greaseproof or non-stick paper and cut it out. Colour another 185g (6oz) sugarpaste red. Thinly roll out half. Lay the template on the sugarpaste and cut around it to shape a truck. Dampen the underside, then secure the truck to the side of the

cake above the green strip. Make and secure more trucks.

6 Shape the remaining red sugarpaste into a solid rectangle and cut out a wedge to form a truck shape.

7 Colour another 125g (4oz) sugarpaste brown. Shape into a thick semi-circle, and cut out the centre with a knife or round cutter to shape a bridge.

8 Colour a little more sugarpaste pale blue. Roll out and position on top of the cake. Arrange the bridge over the blue 'water'. Shape a small path from brown trimmings and secure to the top of the cake. Secure the truck on top of the cake, raising it off the cake slightly on a piece of red sugarpaste trimmings.

9 Colour a little more sugarpaste black and shape into wheels. Secure to all the trucks.

10 Shape tiny balls of green sugarpaste from trimmings, and arrange in rings on the top of the cake. Press candles into the centres, or fill the centres with a dot of red icing. Shape small yellow 'headlights' and secure to the front of the truck.

COOK'S HINT
The simple design of this cake is very effective. However, you could add more detail, such as windows and number plates on the trucks.

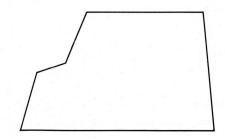

Cut out a wedge to shape the truck. Cut small discs of black sugarpaste for wheels.

Baby Dinosaur Cake

A baby dinosaur, just hatched from its egg, provides an interesting and fun variation on the current craze for anything prehistoric.

Serves 16

CAKE
Madeira cake mixture for 20cm (8 inch) round tin (see page 2)
2.3 litre (4 pint) ovenproof mixing bowl

FILLING AND DECORATION
1.5kg (3lb) Sugarpaste (see page 3)
cornflour for dusting
blue, black, orange, green and red food colourings
6 tbsp strawberry or raspberry jam
125g (4oz / ½ cup) Buttercream (see page 3)

EQUIPMENT
several Easter egg moulds in various sizes
fine paintbrush
33cm (13 inch) round silver cake board
large paintbrush

1 Preheat the oven to 160°C (325°F/ Gas 3). Grease and line the base of the mixing bowl. Make up the Madeira cake mixture, turn it into the bowl and level the surface. Bake in the oven for 1¼ hours or until firm. Turn out on to a wire rack and leave to cool. Wrap tightly in foil and store until required.

2 To make the 'egg shells', lightly knead 500g (1lb) of the sugarpaste. Cover the outside of four or five Easter egg moulds with plastic food wrap. Roll out a little of the sugarpaste on a surface dusted with cornflour, and lay it over one of the moulds. Using the tip of a sharp knife, cut a zig-zag line across the sugarpaste towards one end of the mould, then trim off the excess around the base.

3 Reroll the trimmings and shape several more shells. For small pieces of shell, mark the zig-zag line across the centre of the mould so that both halves can be used. From the remainder of the 500g (1lb) sugarpaste, shape small whole eggs. Leave the shells to harden for 24 hours. Wrap the remaining sugarpaste in plastic food wrap.

4 Carefully pull away the Easter egg moulds and peel the food wrap away from the sugarpaste. Leave the shells to harden for a further 24–48 hours.

5 Using a fine paintbrush and diluted blue and black food colourings, paint dots of colour on to the outside of the shells.

6 Level the surface of the cake by cutting off any peak formed during baking so that it sits flat when inverted. Halve the cake horizontally. Reassemble the cake on the board, sandwiching the layers together with 4 tbsp of the jam and the buttercream.

7 Press the remaining jam through a sieve to remove any pieces. Brush over the cake.

8 Colour another 750g (1½lb) of the sugarpaste orange and roll out to a 36cm (14 inch) round. Lightly dampen the edges of the cake board with water. Lay the sugarpaste over the cake and board, and smooth out using hands dusted with cornflour. Trim off the excess.

continued on page 18

Trim off the excess sugarpaste around the base of each Easter egg mould.

9 Colour 125g (4oz) of the remaining sugarpaste dark green. Reserve another small piece of white sugarpaste, about the size of a grape. Reserve 30g (1oz) of the green icing. Knead together the remaining green and white icing until mottled with colour. Shape a small 2.5cm (1 inch) ball of sugarpaste into the baby dinosaur's head. Cut a slit, almost through to the centre, for the mouth, and mark two nostrils with the tip of a knife.

10 Form the remaining green icing into a ball, then gradually roll and pull out one end into a long thin tail. Lightly dampen the centre of the top of the cake, then position the dinosaur's body, pressing down lightly to secure in place. Place the dinosaur's head in position and secure with a little water.

11 While the dinosaur is still soft, tuck two egg shells around it, lifting the dinosaur gently and repositioning it on the edges of the shells to secure in place. Position the remaining shells and eggs around the cake.

12 Shape and position two small white balls for the dinosaur's eyes. Shape and position a small red tongue.

13 From the reserved green icing, shape a small 'quiff' of hair and several triangular spikes. Position on the dinosaur's head and along the body and tail. Paint the centres of the eyes with black food colouring.

COOK'S HINTS

To make the cake easy to assemble, the 'egg shells' should be made several days in advance. If possible, use Easter egg moulds in various sizes, available from cake-decorating shops. Don't worry if an egg shell cracks during assembly – it all adds to the effect!

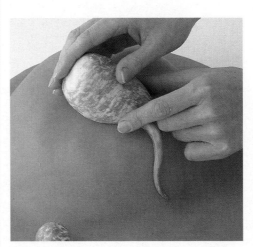

Position the dinosaur on top of the cake before adding any of the egg shell pieces.

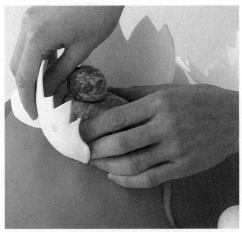

Lift the dinosaur gently and tuck the edge of a piece of shell under each side.

Dream Castle

Fairy-tale castles are always popular with young children. This dreamy creation hides plenty of sweet treasures.

1 Preheat the oven to 160°C (325°F/ Gas 3). Grease and line the base and sides of the round cake tin, and the three food cans (see page 6). Make up the Madeira cake mixture and spoon into the prepared food cans, filling each one two-thirds full. Turn the remaining mixture into the cake tin. Bake the cakes in the oven until firm, allowing about 30 minutes for the cakes in cans, and 1¼ hours for the large cake. Turn out on to a wire rack and leave to cool.

2 Roll out a little sugarpaste on a surface dusted with cornflour and cut out a 7.5cm (3 inch) square. Transfer to a sheet of greaseproof or non-stick paper. Using the tip of a sharp knife, cut out a small archway from one side and notches from the opposite side. Leave to harden for at least 24 hours. Wrap the remaining sugarpaste in plastic food wrap.

3 Place the large cake on the cake board and brush it all over with half the apricot glaze. Roll out 750g (1½lb) of the sugarpaste to a 36cm (14 inch) circle. Lay it over the cake and smooth it around the sides, letting the excess icing overhang the edges of the board. Trim off the excess around the sides of the board so the board around the base of the cake is covered.

4 Level the tops of the small cakes by cutting off any peaks formed during baking. Cut a 2.5cm (1 inch) slice off one cake and secure it with a little apricot glaze to another to make three towers of different sizes. Use a 2.5cm (1 inch) plain round cutter to take a 5cm (2 inch) deep notch out of one side of each of the two tallest towers.

5 Cover the towers with sugarpaste as described on page 26. Place the towers on the cake. Roll out a little sugarpaste, cut out circles and use to cover the tops of the towers. To make windows, cut crosses in the sugarpaste around the towers with a knife, then press the tip of a writer tube into the ends of the arms of each of the crosses.

Serves 20

CAKE
Madeira cake mixture for 23cm (9 inch) round tin (see page 2)
20cm (8 inch) round cake tin
3 empty 400g (14oz) food cans, thoroughly washed and dried

ICING AND DECORATION
1.5kg (3lb) Sugarpaste (see page 2)
cornflour for dusting
6 tbsp Apricot Glaze (see page 3)
pink and yellow food colourings
2 packets of round sherbert sweets
4 sheets of rice, greaseproof or non-stick paper
selection of pastel-coloured sweets
1 egg white
250g (8oz/1½ cups) icing sugar
gold dragees
gold food dusting powder

EQUIPMENT
25cm (10 inch) round silver cake board
2.5cm (1 inch) plain round cutter
medium writer tube
paper piping bag
fine paintbrush

Press the cutter down through the sponge, holding it firmly to keep it straight.

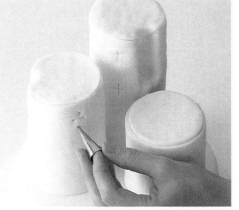

Finish off each 'window' by marking with the point of a writer tube.

6 Roll out two 5cm (2 inch) squares of sugarpaste. Arrange a line of sweets down the centre of each. Wrap the icing around the sweets to cover them. Dampen one edge and secure the ends. Dampen the notched corners on the two towers, then press the mini-towers into position, with the joins facing inwards. Make windows in the mini-towers.

7 Peel the paper away from the hardened archway of icing and secure it against the front towers. Make two more mini-towers and place one at each end of the archway. Leave to harden for several hours or overnight.

8 Cut an 18cm (7 inch) round of rice, greaseproof or non-stick paper into two semi-circles, and shape into cones. Make a third cone from another round of paper. Pile sweets on top of each tower, then dampen the top edges of the towers. Gently rest the cones in position. Make smaller cones from 2.5cm (1 inch) rounds of paper for the mini-towers.

9 Beat the egg white in a bowl, then gradually add the icing sugar to make a paste which forms soft peaks. Place in a paper piping bag fitted with a medium writer tube, and pipe a dot on top of each cone. Top with a gold dragee.

10 Roll out 2cm (¾ inch) strips of sugarpaste. Cut out notches and secure a strip around each tower with the notched edge uppermost. Place thinner notched strips around the mini-towers.

11 Dilute some yellow food colouring with water, then use a fine paintbrush to paint the lower third of each tower and each notched strip. Paint the lower area of the large cake. Dilute some pink food colouring and use to paint the remaining areas of the towers.

12 Using a dry paintbrush, dust the cones and white areas of the lower cake with gold dusting powder. Colour the remaining sugarpaste pale pink and shape into small boulders. Position around the base of the cake.

The mini-towers are positioned in the notches made in the tall towers.

Any suitable sweets can be used in the mini-towers and under the cones.

Bunny Cake

A perfect idea for the tinies! Finished with simply moulded rabbits and cut-out grass, this cake is assembled in no time at all.

1 Level the surface of the cake by cutting off any peak that formed during baking, then cut the cake horizontally in half. Place one layer on the cake board and spread with 4 tbsp of the jam. Cover with the buttercream, then position the second layer on top.

2 Press the remaining jam through a sieve to remove any pieces. Brush the cake with the jam.

3 Colour 1.1kg (2¼lb) of the sugarpaste yellow. Roll out on a surface dusted with cornflour, and use to cover the cake (see page 5).

4 Colour another 125g (4oz) sugarpaste green. Thinly roll out a little and cut out a 13 × 2.5cm (5 × 1 inch) strip. Make cuts down one long side of the strip, through to the centre. Dampen the uncut edge of the strip with water, then lay it against the base of the cake so that the cut edge falls away from the cake to resemble grass. Make more strips and attach all around the base of the cake.

5 Colour another 60g (2oz) sugarpaste pale pink and roll it out thinly. Cut into 13cm × 5mm (5 × ¼ inch) strips, reserving the trimmings. Lightly dampen the points around the top edge of the cake. Gently twist a pink strip and secure it between two points on top of the cake. Repeat all around the cake. Secure small balls of white sugarpaste at the points where the strips meet.

6 To shape a simple 'bunny', start by rolling a piece of white sugarpaste into a ball, about 2.5cm (1 inch) in diameter, for the body. Add a head, ears and a tail. Secure on the centre of the cake. Shape and secure three smaller bunnies. Add small noses and centres of ears using pink icing trimmings. Paint faint features on the bunnies, using a fine paintbrush and diluted black food colouring.

7 Make more grass as described in step 4, but cut into 2.5cm (1 inch) lengths and roll into 'tufts'. Secure the grass and flower decorations to the top of the cake.

Stick the uncut edge of each strip to the cake so the snipped 'grass' falls outwards.

Patch

This endearing little pup will appeal to most young children, particularly if it bears any resemblance to a family pet.

Serves 8

CAKE

Madeira cake mixture for 15cm (6 inch) round tin (see page 2)
3.4 litre (6 pint) ovenproof mixing bowl

ICING AND DECORATION

1 tbsp cocoa powder, sifted
500g (1lb/2 cups) Butter-cream (see page 3)
60g (2oz) Sugarpaste (see Cook's Hint)
black food colouring
3 liquorice 'bootlaces'
15cm (6 inches) ribbon, about 1cm (½ inch) wide
1 chocolate coin

EQUIPMENT

30cm (12 inch) round gold or silver cake board
palette knife
cocktail stick
fine paintbrush

COOK'S HINT

As only a little sugarpaste is required for this cake, buy a small packet rather than make your own. Tightly wrapped, the remainder will keep for several weeks.

---

1 Preheat the oven to 160°C (325°F/Gas 3). Grease and line the base of the mixing bowl. Make up the Madeira cake mixture, turn it into the bowl and level the surface. Bake in the oven for about 40 minutes or until firm. Turn the cake out of the bowl on to a wire rack and leave to cool.

2 Level the surface of the cake by cutting off any peak that formed during baking, so that the cake sits flat when inverted on to the cake board. Beat the cocoa powder into a third of the buttercream.

3 Reserve 3 tbsp of the plain buttercream, then spread the remainder over the cake, covering it as smoothly as possible. Spread a little buttercream on to the board at the bottom of the cake, and build it up to form a 'neck'. Gently fluff up the surface of the buttercream with the tip of a cocktail stick.

4 Spoon the reserved plain buttercream on to the cake in a mound just below the centre, and spread it into a snout shape. Dampen the palette knife, and then smooth down the snout area to contrast with the fluffed-up surface of the rest of the buttercream.

5 Spread a little of the chocolate buttercream over one eye area of the cake. Shape two white eyes from the sugarpaste and position on the cake, placing one over the area of chocolate buttercream.

6 Colour a small piece of sugarpaste black and shape it into a nose. Press gently into position.

7 Arrange pieces of liquorice 'bootlace' around the eyes, pressing them gently into the buttercream. Form a smiling mouth from a little more liquorice.

8 Spread small spoonfuls of the chocolate buttercream down each side of the dog's face. Flatten with a palette knife, widening at the base to shape ears. Fluff up lightly with a cocktail stick. Secure more liquorice around the ears.

9 Paint the centres of the eyes black with food colouring and a fine paintbrush. Arrange the ribbon around the base of the cake, securing the gold coin on it with a dot of buttercream.

Use a palette knife to shape the chocolate buttercream for Patch's ears.

Messy Paints

When lack of time prevents you from creating 'fiddly' cakes, a set of messy paint pots provides a welcome alternative.

Serves 12

CAKE
Madeira cake mixture for 18cm (7 inch) round tin (see page 2)
3 empty 400g (14oz) food cans, thoroughly washed and dried

ICING AND DECORATION
3 tbsp Apricot Glaze (see page 3)
1kg (2lb) Sugarpaste (see page 3)
cornflour for dusting
black, red, blue, green and silver food colourings
500g (1lb/3 cups) icing sugar

EQUIPMENT
large paintbrush
41 × 25cm (16 × 10 inch) silver cake card

COOK'S HINTS
If you can't get a large enough cake card, use a plain coloured tray. For a personal touch, add the child's name and age in the coloured icings.

---

1 Preheat the oven to 160°C (325°F/ Gas 3). Grease and line the food cans (see page 6). Make up the Madeira cake mixture, divide it between the cans and level the surfaces. Bake in the oven for about 30 minutes or until firm. Turn the cakes out of the cans on to a wire rack and leave to cool.

2 Level the tops of the cakes by cutting off any peaks formed during baking. Brush the cakes with apricot glaze. Dampen the cake card.

3 Thinly roll out 185g (6oz) of the sugarpaste on a surface dusted with cornflour. Lay over one side of the cake card, then trim, at an angle, to a square. Thinly roll out another 185g (6oz) sugarpaste and lay over the other side of the board, overlapping the first piece. Trim to a square, cutting around the first piece to resemble sheets of paper. Use trimmings to shape more pieces of paper showing beneath the large sheets.

4 Colour a small piece of sugarpaste, about the size of a grape, with black food colouring. Roll into a ball, then pull to a point for the tip of the brush.

5 Colour the remaining sugarpaste pale grey using black colouring. Reserve 60g (2oz), then divide the remainder into three. Roll out one piece and trim to a 23 × 11.5cm (9 × 4½ inch) rectangle. Wrap one cake in the icing so that the base is in line with one long edge of the icing.

6 Stand the cake vertically on the white icing. Cover the remaining cakes in the same way and position on the board.

7 Roll the reserved grey icing into a paintbrush handle and lay it on the white icing. Secure the black tip in position.

8 Divide the icing sugar between three bowls. Add enough cold water to each to make a paste that becomes level when left to stand for several seconds. Colour one red, one blue and one green.

9 Spoon the red icing on to one pot, 'spilling' plenty down the sides and over the card. Repeat with the remaining colours. Using a large paintbrush dipped in the coloured icings, paint simple shapes on to the white background. Paint the end of the paintbrush with a little silver food colouring.

Before covering, line up the base of each cake with one long edge of the sugarpaste.

Wallet

Gold and silver chocolate coins are now available from supermarkets most of the year. Tumbling out of a simply moulded 'wallet', they make an effective cake for an older child.

Serves 12

CAKE
*Madeira cake mixture for 15cm (6 inch) square tin (see page 2)
23cm (9 inch) square cake tin*

ICING AND DECORATION
*4 tbsp Apricot Glaze (see page 3)
1.5kg (3lb) Sugarpaste (see page 3)
black, brown and gold food colourings
cornflour for dusting
football or other collecting cards
1 bag gold chocolate coins
1 bag silver chocolate coins*

EQUIPMENT
*30cm (12 inch) square gold cake board
polythene bag
fine paintbrush*

1 Preheat the oven to 160°C (325°F/ Gas 3). Grease and line the cake tin. Make up the cake mixture, turn it into the tin and level the surface. Bake in the oven for about 40 minutes or until firm. Turn out on to a wire rack and leave to cool.

2 Level the surface of the cake by cutting off any peak that formed during baking. Invert the cake on to the cake board, and brush with apricot glaze.

3 Colour 1.1kg (2¼lb) of the sugarpaste grey using black food colouring. Roll it out on a surface dusted with cornflour and use to cover the cake (see page 5).

4 Colour the remaining sugarpaste brown. Roll out two-thirds and cut out a 20cm (8 inch) square. Lay this over the cake.

5 Crumple up a polythene bag, then slightly uncrumple it and lay it on top of the brown icing. Roll lightly with a rolling pin to give the icing a textured finish. Remove the bag. Using a knife, make several horizontal cuts down one side of the wallet and insert the cards.

6 Scatter some coins over the other side of the icing, then dampen the edges of the sugarpaste with water. Roll more brown icing to a 21 × 10cm (8¼ × 4 inch) rectangle. Use the polythene bag to texture it in the same way, then lay it over the coins, pressing the edges gently together to secure.

7 Paint the teeth of a zip along the edge of the icing. Shape a small zip end from trimmings, position this on the cake and paint it gold.

8 Using black food colouring, paint 'stitches' around the wallet.

COOK'S HINT
Before inserting the cards, dust them with cornflour so they can easily be pulled out before the cake is cut.

Excess cornflour can easily be brushed off with a paintbrush.

Lay the icing lightly over the coins, then press round the edges to seal.

Pretty Heart

Decorated with a simple tulle 'flounce' and pink hearts, this cake will appeal to girls who love 'pretty' cakes.

Serves 12

CAKE
Madeira cake mixture for 18cm (7 inch) round tin (see page 2)
18cm (7 inch) heart-shaped cake tin

FILLING AND DECORATION
250g (8oz/1 cup) Buttercream (see page 3)
1.5kg (3lb) Sugarpaste (see page 3)
cornflour for dusting
2 metres (2¼ yards) pink or white tulle, about 15cm (6 inches) wide
pink food colouring
silver dragees
66cm (26 inches) silver ribbon, about 2.5cm (1 inch) wide
1 tbsp icing sugar
candles (optional)

EQUIPMENT
palette knife
23cm (9 inch) heart-shaped or round silver cake board or cake card
cocktail stick
small heart-shaped cutters, preferably in two sizes
fine paintbrush

1 Preheat the oven to 160°C (325°F/ Gas 3). Grease and line the base and sides of the cake tin. Make up the Madeira cake mixture, turn it into the tin and level the surface. Bake in the oven for about 1¼ hours or until firm. Turn out on to a wire rack and leave to cool.

2 Level the surface of the cake by cutting off any peak formed during baking. Cut the cake horizontally in half, then sandwich back together with half the buttercream. Place the cake on the board. Using a palette knife, spread with the remaining buttercream.

3 Thinly roll out 375g (12oz) of the sugarpaste on a surface dusted with cornflour. Cut out a 30cm (12 inch) strip and secure it to one half of the cake. Cut out another 30cm (12 inch) strip and secure it to the other side of the cake. Dampen the sugarpaste around the base of the cake.

4 Fold the tulle almost in half. Lay it against the base of the cake with the narrow half uppermost and the fold against the base of the cake. Using the tip of a cocktail stick, tuck the fold of the tulle just under the base of the cake, gathering the tulle slightly as you work. Complete all around the base of the cake.

5 Colour 125g (4oz) sugarpaste pink and reserve. Roll out the remainder to a 30cm (12 inch) circle. Lift this over the cake and let the sugarpaste fall around the sides. Lightly arrange the icing around the sides so that it falls in soft folds but doesn't crush the tulle. Trim off any excess.

6 Thinly roll out the pink sugarpaste and cut out heart shapes. Secure to the top of the cake and to the tulle using a dampened paintbrush. Lightly press silver dragees on top of the cake, if necessary using a dampened paintbrush to secure them. Scatter more around the tulle.

7 To secure the ribbon around the cake, make a paste by mixing the icing sugar and a dash of water. Wrap the ribbon around the cake and secure the ends to the cake with a dot of the paste. Place candles on top of the cake, if required.

COOK'S HINT
If you can't get hold of a heart-shaped tin, use a 20cm (8 inch) round cake and cut out the top and point of the heart. Alternatively, use a round cake – the effect will be just as pretty.

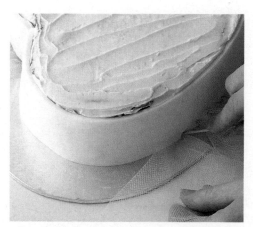

Use a cocktail stick to push the folded edge of tulle under the cake.

Fishing Trip

A simple cake to draw the attention of any budding young fisherman.

Serves 20

CAKE
23cm (9 inch) round Madeira cake (see page 2)

FILLING AND DECORATION
7 tbsp raspberry or strawberry jam
250g (8oz / 1 cup) Buttercream (see page 3)
1.5kg (3lb) Sugarpaste (see page 3)
blue, brown, red, green and yellow food colourings
cornflour for dusting
1 metre (39 inches) green ribbon, about 1cm (½ inch) wide

EQUIPMENT
28cm (11 inch) round silver cake board
fine paintbrush
cocktail sticks
small piece of thread
paper piping bag
medium writer tube

> COOK'S HINT
> *Make the boy in his boat at least 24 hours before assembling the cake to allow time for it to harden.*

1 Level the surface of the cake by cutting off any peak formed during baking, and cut the cake horizontally in half. Spread the bottom layer with 4 tbsp of the jam. Reserve 2 tbsp of the buttercream and spread the remainder over the jam. Cover with the top cake layer and place the cake on the cake board.

2 Press the remaining jam through a sieve to remove any pieces, then brush the jam over the top and sides of the cake.

3 Colour 1kg (2lb) of the sugarpaste blue. Roll it out on a surface dusted with cornflour and use to cover the cake (see page 5).

4 Colour another 60g (2oz) sugarpaste brown. Thinly roll out a little and cut out a leaf shape 7.5cm (3 inches) long and 2.5cm (1 inch) at its widest point. Cut two strips of brown sugarpaste, each 10cm (4 inches) long and 2cm (¾ inch) wide. Dampen the edges of the leaf shape, then secure the strips around it, pinching the ends together to resemble the sides of a boat. Trim off any excess at the ends. Place on a piece of greaseproof or non-stick paper.

5 Colour another 60g (2oz) icing pink using a dot of red colouring. Roll a small ball for the boy's head. Shape a 9cm (3½ inch) sausage from the remaining pink icing, tapering it at the ends. Cut a 2.5cm (1 inch) slit from each end towards the centre. Open out one end and shape to resemble bent arms; cross the pieces at the other end for legs. Place in the boat, resting the head on the arms. (If necessary, prop up the sides of the boat with crumpled absorbent kitchen paper while the sugarpaste hardens.)

6 Colour another 250g (8oz) sugarpaste green. Thinly roll it out, and cut out leaves in various sizes. Using a dampened paintbrush, secure them all around the sides of the cake.

7 Press several cocktail sticks at intervals into the sides of the cake. Thread a small sausage of brown icing over the end of each for bulrushes.

8 Once the boy in the boat has hardened, paint on clothes using different colourings and a fine paintbrush. If liked, add icing hair, a hat, boots, book, etc. Secure the boat to the cake.

9 Push a cocktail stick into the base of the boat for a fishing rod. Tie a length of thread to the end for a dangling line. Paint the rod brown or red. From the remaining icing, shape small fish heads and position on the water. A small piece of sugarpaste can be shaped and placed on the fishing rod to resemble a reel.

10 Place the reserved buttercream in a piping bag fitted with a medium writer tube, and pipe ripples of water around the line, the fish and the boat.

11 Wrap the ribbon around the base of the cake, securing with a little buttercream.

Position the boy's head as if resting on his arms as he lies in the boat.

Sunny Valley Farm

A lovely cake for a small child. The decorations can be as simple or as detailed as you like, depending on time and patience.

Serves 16

CAKE
18cm (7 inch) square Madeira cake (see page 2)

ICING AND DECORATION
750g (1½lb/3 cups) Buttercream (see page 3)
500g (1lb) Sugarpaste (see page 3)
brown, blue and green food colourings
cornflour for dusting
bought sugar flowers
2 shredded wheat
plastic farm animals, e.g. horses, sheep, ducks, chickens

EQUIPMENT
palette knife
33cm (13 inch) round silver cake board
2 paper piping bags
medium writer tube

> **COOK'S HINT**
> *A bag of cheap plastic farm animals is ideal for this cake. Try to find one that includes sections of plastic fencing.*

---

1 Level the surface of the cake by cutting off any peak that formed during baking. Cut the cake vertically in half, then sandwich the two pieces together again, side by side, with a little buttercream. Cut the two top edges off each side and secure to the top of the cake with buttercream to shape the roof.

2 Position the cake to one side of the cake board. Using a palette knife, cover all sides of the cake with a little buttercream, spreading it as smoothly as possible. Using a knife, make brick markings around the sides.

3 Colour half the sugarpaste brown and roll it out on a surface dusted with cornflour. Cut out small squares and use to 'tile' the roof. Reserve the trimmings. Colour more sugarpaste blue, roll it out and cut out small windows, reserving the trimmings. Press the windows into position. Use the brown trimmings to make shutters and a door.

4 Reserve 4 tbsp of the buttercream and colour the remainder green. Place 2 tbsp green buttercream in a paper piping bag fitted with a medium writer tube, then spread the remainder over the cake board, mounding up the buttercream in places to create small 'hills'. Lightly roll out the blue sugarpaste trimmings and press on to the buttercream for a pond.

5 Colour 2 tbsp of the remaining buttercream brown and spread across the centre of the board for a mud track.

6 Use the green buttercream in the piping bag to pipe trailing greenery up the sides of the house and on the roof. Secure the sugar flowers.

7 Clean the tube and fit inside a new paper piping bag. Fill with plain buttercream and use to pipe ripples on the pond, windowpanes and blossom.

8 Lightly break up the shredded wheat and tie in bundles with a little thinly rolled brown sugarpaste. Arrange in a stack.

9 Arrange the plastic fencing and farm animals around the cake.

Make sure you keep the knife blade straight as you cut through the cake.

Arrange the cake pieces with cut sides facing out to form the top of the roof.

Café

This is a lovely cake to make if you enjoy small-scale modelling. The idea also lends itself to several other themes, such as a sweetshop or market stall.

Serves 20

CAKE
20cm (8 inch) square Madeira cake (see page 2)

FILLING AND DECORATION
8 tbsp strawberry or raspberry jam
1.5kg (3lb) Sugarpaste (see page 3)
cornflour for dusting
red, black, yellow, green, blue and silver food colourings
1 sheet of leaf gelatine
125g (4oz / ¾ cup) icing sugar chocolate vermicelli

EQUIPMENT
30cm (12 inch) round silver cake board
large paintbrush
fine paintbrush
paper piping bag
medium writer tube
2cm (¾ inch) and 1cm (½ inch) plain round cutters

1 Level the surface of the cake by cutting off any peak that formed during baking, then split the cake horizontally into three. Sandwich the cake layers back together with 6 tbsp of the strawberry or raspberry jam. Halve the cake vertically and stand each piece on its side.

2 Brush the cake board with a little water. Thinly roll out 315g (10oz) of the sugarpaste on a surface dusted with cornflour and lay it over the cake board. Smooth the icing with hands dusted with cornflour, and trim off the excess around the sides.

3 Using a large knife, mark lines across the sugarpaste, 2.5cm (1 inch) apart, then mark lines in the opposite direction to make squares. Using a fine paintbrush and diluted red food colouring, paint alternate squares to give the board a chequered appearance.

4 Press the remaining jam through a sieve to remove any pieces. Brush over the top and sides of the cake, then position the cakes 2.5cm (1 inch) apart on the chequered board.

5 Partially knead a dot of black food colouring into 125g (4oz) sugarpaste so that the icing is marbled with colour (see page 4). Thinly roll it out and cut out two 20 × 5cm (8 × 2 inch) rectangles. Lay one on the top of each cake.

6 Colour another 500g (1lb) sugarpaste pale yellow. Roll it out and cut it into 9.5cm (3¾ inch) wide strips. Trim the ends, and then position around the sides of the cakes, pinching up the edges to gather. Use more strips until all the sides are covered with icing. While the paste is still soft, lift part of one side up and support it so that it will dry in that position, enabling the cat to be positioned later.

7 Mould a little white sugarpaste into a cylindrical shape and position it at one end of one counter for the urn. Roll and shape several small white trays, each measuring 4 × 2.5cm (1½ × 1 inch).

continued on page 38

Marking guidelines in the sugarpaste makes painting alternate squares simple.

Gather the sugarpaste around the top as you secure it.